CHURCH UNITY
SERIES

*A Divided
House
Cannot Stand*

D1547651

BY

WISDOM

THE HOUSE

IS BUILT

*Truths compiled
from the writings of*

**FRANCIS
FRANGIPANE**

ISBN #1-886296-07-3

Copyright © 1994 Francis Frangipane
Arrow Publications
P.O. Box 10102
Cedar Rapids, IA 52410

CONTENTS

chapters from *The House of the Lord*

1.

BY WISDOM THE HOUSE IS BUILT

The Fear of the Lord

There was a small city with few men in it and a great king came to it, surrounded it, and constructed large siegeworks against it. But there was found in it a poor wise man and he delivered the city by his wisdom" (Eccl 9:14-15).

The wisdom of God can take even a poor man, train him in the ways of the Lord and give him a strategy to deliver a city. Throughout the ages the Lord has had His judges, generals and kings who have delivered the nation of Israel. In more modern times God has had His Wesleys, His Martin Luthers, His Jonathan Edwardses—men who turned their countries toward heaven. The chaos of our cities is not greater than the chaos which covered the deep, formless, primeval void. God's wisdom brought creation into order, and His wisdom can bring the church back to order as well.

The Lord desires for you to possess His wisdom. How do you find it? **"The fear of the Lord is the beginning of wisdom, and the knowledge of the Holy One is understanding"** (Prov 9:10). What is **"the fear of the Lord"**? It is the human soul, having experienced the crucifixion of self and pride, now trembling in stark vulnerability before almighty God. It is this living awareness: God sees everything. This penetrating discovery marks the holy beginning of finding true wisdom.

However, this perception of the living God is not a terrible reality, for it liberates the mind from the cocoon of carnality, enabling the soul to escape into the Spirit. For all the dynamic gifts through which Jesus revealed the Father's power, His delight was in the fear of the Lord (see Isaiah 11:1-3). Yes, it is the awe-inspiring wonder of man living in fellowship, not with his religion, but with his God. In such a state the obedient man is invincible.

Indeed, has this not been our problem: The enemy does not fear the church because the church does not fear the Lord? As the fear of the Lord returns to us, the terror of the Lord will be upon our enemies. The fear of the Lord is our wisdom.

Let Wisdom Guide Your Building

"By wisdom a house is built, and by understanding it is established; and by knowledge the rooms are filled with all precious and pleasant riches" (Prov 24:3-4). The Lord's house is built by wisdom. It is established as we compassionately seek to understand the needs of our brethren. After it is built and established, then knowledge fills the rooms with riches.

You may be asking, Where do I begin? James tells us that if we lack wisdom, we can **"ask of God"** (James 1:5). Proverbs 4:7 tells us, **"The beginning of wisdom is: Acquire wisdom."** Wisdom is within the grasp of every man. Ask for wisdom but seek the Lord, for with Him there is sound wisdom stored up for the upright.

Do not panic if wisdom seems far from you. Jesus Himself **"kept increasing in wisdom"** (Luke 2:52). Ultimately those who knew Him marveled, wondering, **"What is this wisdom given to Him?"** (Mark 6:2) Jesus grew in wisdom, and so also shall you.

God's Manifold Wisdom

It is the everlasting purpose of God that through the church His **"manifold wisdom"** might be known **"unto the principalities and powers in heavenly places"** (Eph 3:10 KJV). Yes, the Lord has instructed us concerning love. Truly He has apportioned to us an effectual measure of faith. Now He desires to give to His church wisdom.

However, the above scripture speaks of the **"manifold"** wisdom of God. There are "many folds" to the wisdom of God. Moreover, there is a difference between knowledge and wisdom. We certainly will perish for a lack of knowledge (see Hosea 4:6), but knowledge by itself only puffs up (see 1 Corinthians 8:1-2). Wisdom knows what to speak and when to speak it. Knowledge, especially doctrinal knowledge, must be administered through wisdom. Presented by itself even knowledge about unity can be divisive.

Oh, how the church desperately needs men and women in whose mind dwells the wisdom of God, a people who are intimately obedient to the ways of God! We have tried zeal, human ingenuity and ambitious programs, but to little avail. We have endured, but not overcome as we had envisioned. Now it is time for those who lack wisdom to ask of God and receive liberally from Him the wisdom to build His house.

The Proper Emphasis of Doctrines

There are doctrines without which we cannot be saved, and there are doctrines which are of lesser importance. "Jesus is Lord" is an unalterable doctrine. "Christ died for sinners" is another. "Jesus Himself is returning" is still another tenet that is essential to true Christian life.

But *when* Jesus returns, whether pre-tribulation, mid-tribulation or post-tribulation, is of lesser importance. As Jesus said, **"Be on the alert—for you do not know when the master of the house is coming, whether in the evening, at midnight, at cockcrowing, or in the morning"** (Mark 13:35). It simply is not wisdom to argue and divide over when He will return, but rather to remain on the alert.

Defining our doctrines is important. We need to clarify our belief systems so our perceptions of truth might be divinely structured and overlaid correctly upon the Scriptures. Without such organization we have little hope of attaining the full benefits of our salvation. However, we can have all the right doctrines and still live outside the presence of God if our hearts are not right. Jesus said, **"By this all men will know that you are My disciples, if you have love for one another"** (John 13:35).

The outcome of right doctrines is love—love that covers other Christians and builds up the body of Christ; it forgives when offended and serves without hidden motives. It goes extra miles ungrudgingly. If our doctrines are not producing this kind of love, they are a smoke screen that will keep us separate and outside the house of the Lord. Let me give an example. In the first-century church there was a controversy concerning eating meat sacrificed to idols. Paul had his views, while others had theirs (see 1 Corinthians 8:8; Acts 15:29; Revelation 2:20). But when he wrote on this subject, he said, **"Now concerning things sacrificed to idols, we know that we all have knowledge. Knowledge makes arrogant, but love edifies"** (1 Cor 8:1).

Paul put love *above* knowledge. Everyone had a doctrine or conviction on the subject. In another epistle, Paul prayed that the Ephesians would **"know the love of Christ which surpasses knowledge"** (Eph 3:19). The love of Christ **"surpasses knowledge."** Even as Jesus bears with our ignorance because of love, so we must set our priorities according to His love and overlook that which will be more easily communicated as our relationships mature.

It is true that without knowledge we will perish, but knowledge without love is itself a state of perishing. Therefore, to build the right foundation of the city-church, we must all be in agreement about Jesus and His command to love one another. Greater wisdom than this will not be given concerning building the house of the Lord.

The Wisdom from Above

There are realistic steps toward seeing prayer and the house of the Lord established in your area. If wisdom shall build the house, it is important to define this dimension of Christ's nature. James 3:17 tells us **"the wisdom from above is first pure."** We cannot build the Lord's house with selfish or ambitious motives. Our desire should be to see the Lord satisfied. Therefore, our labors must be for Jesus, not self. It must be the love of Christ which compels us, not a desire to rise in prominence among men.

Divine wisdom is next **"peaceable"** (James 3:17). Peacemakers are sons of God; they are men and women of wisdom. Their wisdom lies in their understanding of the sublime and powerful ways of God. This wisdom is not born merely of intellectual study. Rather, because they have accepted the Lord's reproof, truth dwells in their innermost beings. The same eternal voice which brought correction **"in the hidden part"** is now rewarding them, granting them to **"know wisdom"** (Ps 51:6).

The wisdom from above is also gentle and reasonable. We must be more willing to serve than to lead, more willing to be corrected than to teach. Where we see a need such as in the areas of initiating prayer or administration, we should be given to fill the gap. But we must also be quick to surrender our task to any whom the Lord raises without feeling as though we have failed because another more qualified has arrived.

True wisdom is not stubborn but is willing to yield to other ministries and perspectives. It must be unyielding in regard to the deity and centrality of Christ and yet fully aware that God desires all men to be saved, **"with gentleness correcting those who are in opposition, if perhaps God may grant them repentance"** (2 Tim 2:25).

While the wisdom of God is meek, it is also **"unwavering, without hypocrisy"** (James 3:17). This is wisdom born out of vision, not organizational skills. It is unwavering because it sees that the builder of the house is Christ. It is genuine, **"full of mercy and good fruits"** (v 17), overlooking mistakes, helping the weaker churches, disarming suspicion and fear with the credibility of Christ's unfailing love.

Dear Lord, You promised that if we lacked wisdom, You would give it to us liberally. We fear being trapped in our own ways with our own ideas. God grant us wisdom, plans and strategies. Grant us the holy fear of Yourself, that You would become to us wisdom, knowledge and strength. In Jesus' name. Amen.

2.

THE ANOINTING TO BUILD

Working with the Holy Spirit, citywide church leaders are receiving the Lord's concern for the entire living church in their regions. To the degree they are building one body of Christ in their cities, they are under the apostolic anointing.

Before we proceed further into this chapter, there are certain apprehensions we want to defuse. The first is that some may think our goal is to build a new denominational structure. This is completely untrue. The zeal which consumes us and the love which compels us is for our Father's house. Our goal, which we believe is God's goal, is to see the born-again church united under the blood of Christ.

It is our perception that the Lord does not want to eliminate denominational relationships nor separate congregations from the heritage of their forefathers. The Lord does not want to eliminate what we each have received, but to integrate it, that light may be given **"to all who are in the house"** (Matt 5:15). We believe God's purpose is not to break off national affiliations, but to heal and establish relationships locally.

We also want to remove any sense of human pressure concerning citywide prayer. The desire to pray with other pastors and churches is a gift which God Himself works into the individual. To pluck this fruit prematurely is to have a crop that is both bitter and hard. Those who embrace citywide prayer should do so because of revelation born of God. To seek to motivate pastors by pressure or manipulation will only breed resentment among them; they will fail to find the sweet pleasure which comes when leaders willingly seek God together. If you are concerned about your pastor, pressure heaven with prayer and then leave this work of grace in the Creator's hands.

To those who are not yet involved, let me assure you: The nature of the born-again, praying church is to appeal to God for you and the rest of the body of Christ. Anyone who exudes an attitude of superiority does not represent our hearts nor the heart of God. In truth, our focus is not on becoming leaders, but followers of Jesus; not on a new doctrine, but on obedience to the directives of Christ. We consider all elitism to be arrogant and an attitude God resists. Religious pride was the first stronghold to fall, enabling us, as pastors from different streams, to flow together. God help us that it not be the first sin to arise in this new stirring of His Spirit!

Our prayer is that we will help you initiate a new and holy beginning of the house of the Lord in your city. Let us also note that if a church recognizes Jesus as Lord and the need to be spiritually reborn; if they hold to the truth of the Scriptures and long for the personal return of the Lord Jesus, then we receive them as our brethren. We recognize that Jesus is not only the way to the Father; He is also the bridge to one another. We present to you no other plan or organization than Christ Himself.

The Apostolic Anointing

The first-century apostles left us more than their words; they also left us their anointing through which we can build the house of the Lord. As we submit to their instructions, and as we are built upon Christ the cornerstone, grace is being granted to build the living house of the Lord.

What is this apostolic anointing? In the same way a pastor is anointed to care unselfishly for his local congregation, so the apostolic anointing awakens local ministers and intercessors to work together in meeting the needs of the citywide body of Christ. It is a love-motivated awareness that the church is *one,* and when one member suffers we all suffer. We each bear a responsibility for our corporate condition.

However, when we speak of an apostolic anointing, we are not referring to men who are twentieth-century apostles. We have one who is our apostle: Christ, **"the Apostle and High Priest of our confession"** (Heb 3:1). Although invisible, it is He who is guiding, building and setting in order His church. He is with us, even to the end of the age. When we speak of this anointing, we are speaking of a grace coming from Christ the apostle which is settling upon obedient leaders in local Christian churches. Out of His fullness these individuals are beginning to build with apostolic vision.

And what is apostolic vision?

There is one body and one Spirit, just as also you were called in one hope of your calling; one Lord, one faith, one baptism, one God and Father of all who is over all and through all and in all (Eph 4:4-6).

Maintaining Freedom

Those anointed with this fresh oil appreciate and respect the diversity of ministry which is already resident in the leaders of the praying, citywide church. They recognize that God has been work-ing in their lives, teaching and guiding, for a number of years. They also recog-nize that they have received from God an eagerness to pray for and with other pas-tors and are products of the grace of God, who Himself has brought them to a place of usefulness in building the citywide church.

In the next chapter we will speak of the priority to build using Jesus as the model for the church. But there are other priorities we must embrace if we will see the body of Christ healed. Our uniting with other churches must be free of subtle desires for control. In spite of the prob-lem of sin in the ministry, we should beware of setting up a premature or legalistic standard of accountability, lest we cut off the flow of grace to our work.

This first stage is *relational,* where we are more concerned with our brethren's needs than their creeds. Of course, if an individual is practicing obvious sin or teaching blatant heresy, he should be approached according to the Lord's instructions in Matthew 18:15-18. How-ever, our focus is not upon where we have come from, but upon where and toward Whom we are going. After love and friendship are established, correction, in many cases, will take care of itself.

Many in the past have tried to unite the church through governmental or doctrinal conformity. Yet they have failed simply because knowledge, instead of the Lord Jesus Christ, was the centerpiece of their approach. Consequently, even their desire for unity became divisive, for only those of like standards eventually clustered together. At this point, let us maintain the standards we each have received from God without putting any burden other than love upon one another.

"Now the Lord is the Spirit; and where the Spirit of the Lord is, there is liberty" (2 Cor 3:17). I am listing liberty as a vital priority because our spiritual freedom is an evidence of the presence and involvement of the Lord. **"It was for freedom that Christ set us free; therefore keep standing firm and do not be subject again to a yoke of slavery"** (Gal 5:1). Without freedom to maintain differing doctrinal views or procedures, we will only be exchanging an old form of slavery for a new one.

There will be great variety and power released as individuals with contrasting gifts begin to flow together. In Acts 13:1-2 we read of **"prophets and teachers"** who were **"ministering to the Lord and fasting."** Not out of corporate board meetings, but out of corporate prayer and dependency upon the Lord, come divine directives for the church: **"the Holy**

Spirit said, 'Set apart for Me Barnabas and Saul' " (v 2).

Organization is necessary. In fact, **"administrations"** is one of the ministry gifts mentioned by Paul in 1 Corinthians 12:28. However, God has appointed in the church **"first apostles, second prophets, third teachers"** (v 28). There is an order through which administrations function properly. But the organizers must be willing to stay flexible and submissive to the leading of God's anointing.

We all appreciate good administrators who have streamlined operations and facilitated the success of our projects. But if a choice is to be made, it would be better to have leaders who are somewhat disheveled, yet who have hearts passionately addicted to loving God, than administrators who rely only upon human wisdom. Leaders must serve for the sake of communication, not control. They should coordinate ministries of mercy, connecting the hurting with the helping. But they must not be allowed to lead the movement of the city-church independently; that direction must come from the Lord Himself.

Characteristics of Leadership

There are three attitudes of heart that are essential for walking in leadership. The first is our passion for the words of Christ. Without this singular goal, every step we take will be off center and contain a certain element of deception in it.

The second attitude leadership must possess is humility. The Lord tells us through Isaiah, **"Heaven is My throne, and the earth is My footstool. Where then is a house you could build for Me? And where is a place that I may rest?"** (Isa 66:1). Humility tells us that no amount of our ingenuity, manipulation, or money could build a house for the Creator. Whatever we build for Him has a measure of idolatry in it; we ultimately find ourselves worshipping the works of our hands.

However, the Lord *is* speaking here of His house; and He is giving us a clear direction into its nature. He says, **"But to this one I will look, to him who is humble and contrite of spirit, and who trembles at My word"** (Isa 66:2). Brokenness, a repentant heart and a holy, trembling fear of God are the building materials of the house of the Lord. It is the Lord's building—a place where He can rest.

Apostolic Prayer

The third attitude of anointed leadership is prayer. While we are indeed seeking to see our cities renewed, the kingdom of God is not a social program. It is only as Christ Himself is established in the church that the city can be divinely impacted. When He is lifted up, men are drawn to Him.

Therefore, the thrust of much of our prayer is toward Christ and fellowship with Him. The essence of prayer is a yearning for Jesus. It would be in keeping with the highest purposes of God that entire prayer meetings be devoted to seeking the Lord. Covet such times, for with them the Lord is well-pleased.

Apostolic prayer can also be called "birthing prayer." Paul taught, **"My children, with whom I am again in labor until Christ is formed in you"** (Gal 4:19). There are dimensions in the ministry of the church that will not come forth until intercessors pray in the power of this apostolic birthing of the church.

Those under this anointing will be so inflamed with a passion for justice that the Lord will lead them into extended periods of fasting and prayer. An anointed few will even be graced to fast publicly for their region. Many cities will be brought to deep repentance. In some cases not only will abortion be outlawed, but even the cause of abortions (illegitimate pregnancies) will begin to cease. The promise of the Lord is, **"Blessed are those who hunger and thirst for righteousness, for they shall be satisfied"** (Matt 5:6).

Apostolic intercession also assumes a posture of spiritual responsibility to support and protect what is newly born and vulnerable. It does not judge the standards of the prayer group, but prays for increase in maturity. It is committed to be an example of spiritual maturity in that process.

As this ministry grows, there will be those upon whose "prayer shoulders" God places the burden for their cities. They will not and cannot sleep without praying for their communities. They assume a place of responsibility for the condition of the region. They will see a direct correlation between personal prayer and the retreat of the enemy from their cities.

One may question such an office; however, it is not unlike the ministry Martin Luther carried in Germany. He said, "If I miss prayer one day, I feel it; if I fail to pray two days, the entire church feels it; should I not pray three days, all Germany suffers."

The Lord is raising up ministers who are spiritually responsible for their churches and their cities. They will not let a day pass without intercession. When they are in battle, they discern the wider range of assault. This is simply a dimension of the apostolic anointing, the gift of spiritual responsibility in prayer.

Dear Lord Jesus, it is our desire to see Your house built. Yet we acknowledge that heaven is Your throne and earth Your footstool; no house we build is worthy or capable of receiving You. Nevertheless, You have promised to build with humble, contrite people who

*tremble when You speak. Lord, help
us maintain freedom and grace. Help
us yield to Your ability to make us a
dwelling place of prayer. By Your grace
we take responsibility for our churches
and our cities. Amen.*

3.

THE STONE THE BUILDERS REJECTED

The goal of God in this new anointing is to return the church to the simplicity and purity of devotion to Christ. The correct foundation is not just what Jesus did in redemption, but what He commands as Lord. Once the foundation is properly laid within us, the house of the Lord can be built.

Becoming Wise Master Builders

Paul said, **"As a wise master builder I laid a foundation"** (1 Cor 3:10). The eternal foundation of the church is the Lord Jesus Christ; we rest and build upon Him. It is wisdom to build the Lord's house with only Jesus in mind, for He must be the central figure of every effort; He must abide as the living source of all our virtue.

Yet there is an unconscious tendency to avoid the teachings of Christ in favor of some other emphasis from the Scriptures. We make our favorite teaching, rather than Jesus, into the cornerstone of our church. Inevitably we find ourselves attempting to make disciples in our image instead of His.

Jesus said, **"The stone which the builders rejected, this became the chief corner stone"** (Luke 20:17). It is important to understand that we cannot separate what Jesus says from Who Jesus is. Christ and His Word are one. To the degree that we fail to teach what Jesus taught, we are actually rejecting Him as Lord and redefining the dimensions of the cornerstone of the church.

Listen to how the Lord associates Himself with His teachings. He said, **"He who rejects Me, and does not receive My sayings, has one who judges him; the word I spoke is what will judge him at the last day"** (John 12:48). He warned, **"Whoever is ashamed of Me and My words, of him will the Son of Man be ashamed when He comes in His glory"** (Luke 9:26). He exposes our hypocrisy, saying, **"Why do you call Me 'Lord,**

Lord,' and do not do what I say?" (Luke 6:46). Christ and His Word are inseparable. Jesus was not a man who became the Word, but is the eternal Word who became a man. His very nature is the Word of God. And to reject or ignore what He says is to reject or ignore who He is.

We cannot build the house of the Lord if we do not honor and build upon the full spectrum of Christ's teachings. Unless we are teaching our converts **"all that [He] commanded,"** we are not making disciples (Matt 28:20); we in our church society will always be trapped in spiritual infancy and religion.

Therefore let us honestly ask ourselves: In the building plan of our churches, how much of an emphasis are we placing upon the words of Jesus? Is there a process in which new converts can become disciples of Christ?

If yours is like many congregations, there is probably little focus given to systematic study and application of Christ's teaching. You see, if Jesus is truly the designer and builder of this house, then we must come to Him for the architectural plans. The building code of the kingdom must be obedience to the words of Christ.

> **"Therefore everyone who hears these words of Mine, and acts upon them, may be compared to a wise man, who built his house upon the rock. And the rain descended, and the floods came,**

and the winds blew, and burst against that house; and yet it did not fall, for it had been founded upon the rock" (Matt 7:24-25).

Beloved, there is a storm coming; even now the sky has darkened and the first drops are falling. If we will endure, we must be built upon the rock. Please hear me: you cannot build your house in a storm. It is through the Spirit and words of Christ that the house of the Lord is built. This is exactly what Jesus meant when He said, **"I will build my church, and the gates of hell shall not prevail against it"** (Matt 16:18 KJV).

The Apostolic Foundation

Multitudes of Christians today know what Jesus did, yet remain stunted in their spiritual growth. Why? Without realizing it, we made the teachings of Paul the cornerstone of the church. The apostle's emphasis centered upon salvation, which faithfully brought us to Jesus. With great wisdom Paul presented God's plan of redemption in Christ. Paul's message revealed what Christ did; but Paul himself was built upon what Christ said. Paul did not become apostle Paul apart from the words of Christ dwelling in him richly.

Yet Jesus alone said He was the way, the truth, and the life. Only His words and Spirit are capable of restructuring our souls so that, through conformity to His nature, the Father Himself can make His abode in us (see John 14:23). It is this refashioning of our inner man that, upon maturity, establishes us corporately as the house of the Lord.

We are not implying that the rest of the Bible is less anointed or pertinent. It is simply that if the cornerstone is not in place the whole building tends to tilt toward the way we happen to lean.

What we are saying about the priority of Christ's words is in full conformity to the apostolic tradition of the New Testament. Paul writes,

If anyone advocates a different doctrine, and does not agree with sound words, those of our Lord Jesus Christ, and with the doctrine conforming to godliness, he is conceited and understands nothing (1 Tim 6:3-4).

When we seek to build upon a foundation other than Jesus, the results are everything but Jesus. Only Christ can create Christians. If we focus on our "doctrinal novelties," seeking to be just different enough to attract more people than the church down the street, we have missed the entire purpose of both the gospel and the ministry of Christ.

Paul based his teaching on **"sound words, those of our Lord Jesus Christ."** Now look at what John taught:

Watch yourselves, that you might not lose what we have accomplished, but that you may receive a full reward. Anyone

who goes too far and does not abide in the teaching of Christ, does not have God (2 John 8-9).

Notes

The priority of this hour is for the church to abide in the teachings and Spirit of the Lord Jesus. From this foundation, the house of the Lord will be built.

We have had our pet doctrines and our own particular emphasis. We have been like Peter speaking to Jesus on the Mount of Transfiguration, **"Lord, it is good for us to be here; if You wish, I will make three tabernacles"** (Matt 17:4). We are so ready to offer a plan to God instead of simply hearing and obeying Jesus. I believe the Father Himself has had enough of our ideas and advice. In His love, He is interrupting our programs with the same word with which He interrupted Peter: **"This is My beloved Son, with whom I am well-pleased; listen to Him!"** (Matt 17:5)

Dear Lord, forgive me for following winds of doctrine instead of picking up my cross and following You. Help me now to return with my whole heart to Your words. Lord, I desire to abide in You. I recommit my life to You, and I pray that You alone would be the focal point of all Your people. In Jesus' name. Amen.

4.

IT TAKES A CITYWIDE CHURCH

Many Christians believe that in the last days the only unity will be in the apostate church. Ironically, it is the very enemy they fear, the Antichrist, that has separated them from other born-again churches in their city! Their aloofness is rooted in self-righteousness. Such an atittude cannot win the war for their cities!

United in Worship and War

One need not be a Bible scholar to recognize that the Jews had to be uncompromisingly united in their worship of God. All Israel was required to come to

Jerusalem three times a year to worship during the feasts. If their worship was compromised, and they were serving the pagan gods of the region, they could not stand in battle. However, in addition to unity in worship, they also had to be united in warfare. Unless they ultimately faced the battle as **"one man,"** their victory was rarely assured (see Judges 6:16; 20:1,8,11; 1 Samuel 11:7; Ezra 3:1).

From the beginning, the Lord has called us to be our brother's keeper. His standard has not changed. Today He is still calling us to cease fighting with one another and to unite in Christ against our common enemies.

There is an Old Testament story which reveals the heart we are seeking. The Israelites were in the land of Gilead, about to cross the Jordan River (see Numbers 32). The tribes of Reuben and Gad, which had amassed much livestock, asked that their inheritance be given first, as the land on which they stood was suitable for grazing. Their request angered Moses for he assumed they sought to divide from the nation in order to gain their individual inheritance.

However, Reuben and Gad had a vision greater than Moses realized. Their words to Moses capture the attitude we must have concerning the other churches in our cities. They said,

> **"We will build here sheepfolds for our livestock and cities for our little ones; but we ourselves**

will be armed ready to go before the sons of Israel, until we have brought them to their place" (Num 32:16-17).

They refused to put down their swords until every tribe had gained its inheritance.

Truly, each church must maintain its individual **"sheepfolds,"** the local fellowship, for the sense of family and continuity. We are compelled by God's love to provide a spiritual shelter to raise our **"little ones."** However, we must also be armed and ready to war on behalf of our brethren.

You see, although we are divided by "tribes" (denominations), we are all part of the same spiritual nation. And while we all have unique battles facing us, our collective and conscious unity under Christ's anointing brings terror to the heart of our enemy. It is this united house of the Lord that will turn our cities to God.

Consequently, in this hour God is raising up strong, seasoned leaders who are equipping their saints to pray and war in behalf of the *other* churches in their city. Intercessors are being trained, not only to protect and defend the citywide church, but to go before them to help secure their inheritance in Christ. Our prayer is that the attitude in Reuben and Gad will become the stance of the mature churches in every city. They said, **"We will not return to our homes until**

**every one of the sons of Israel has pos-
sessed his inheritance"** (Num 32:18).

Our Strategy in Spiritual Warfare

To go successfully before our brethren in war, the Lord Himself must pre-
pare us. If we ignore the Lord's training,
a confrontational posture against the
enemy will be, at best, ineffective and, at
worst, dangerous. If you attempt to "bind"
a principality or power but harbor sin in
your heart, you will certainly be defeated.
We have no authority over a foe *outside*
of us if we are compromising with that
foe *inside* of us. Thus, after discerning a
ruling principality or power over an area,
our first step in warfare is to cleanse the
citywide church of its openness toward
demonic influence. After pulling down
the corresponding strongholds among the
people, we then seek God in order to discern if this is an enemy He is calling us
to confront.

When we were in the Washington,
D.C., area, the Lord revealed that we were
to pray against the power of deceit over
the area. Since deceit was also somewhat
operative in the church, our first act was
to cleanse the participating congregation
of deception. We did so by calling everyone to expose and confess their secret
sins. After breaking the power of deceit
over us, we prayed over the city and sur-
rounding area. That very evening, Marion
Barry, the mayor of Washington, was
arrested for drug use. The media

reported that the police had sought his arrest for years, but he had cloaked himself in deceit.

As in any war, many things must be in place before the Lord will engage the church in confrontational warfare. We must not be anxious to try our new "doctrinal gun" of spiritual warfare, especially if our hearts are not filled with the firepower of Christ Himself.

More often, however, the Lord gives discernment, not for us to engage in warfare, but so that we will be aware of the enemy and be cleansed of his influence. In the initial stages of our training, we will soon discover that the Lord is more concerned with establishing His presence in the church than He is with addressing the regional principalities and powers. For it is not until the nature of Christ is in us, and the voice of Christ is speaking through us, that the Spirit of Christ penetrates the heavenly places, displacing the spiritual darkness over an area.

Suppose, however, that a number of churches are participating, and you have repented and are cleansed of the influence of the specific enemy you seek to confront. How do you engage in warfare? The answer to this question is multifaceted. First, our prayers must be scripturally-based expressions of God's *written* judgment as seen in the Scriptures. The **"sword of the Spirit"** is the **"word of God"** (Eph 6:17). We must never boast about what we will do to the devil. We are servants carrying out God's will through speaking His Word.

Additionally, our prayers are not mere words without corresponding actions. Our prayer of judgment is a representation of our commitment to see the kingdom of God prevail in the very territory Satan held, even if it costs us our lives. In other words, our prayers are backed up by a willingness to die for what we believe in.

Prayer is not our only weapon. Our feet are shod in preparation to speak the gospel. While we war in prayer, we are simultaneously reaching out to people through evangelism, seminars, and publications; through teaching on the radio and television; and, when appropriate, by participating in public demonstrations. You see, although our assault begins in the heavenly places, it extends to many fronts.

"By My Spirit," Says the Lord

Jesus said, **"If I cast out demons by the Spirit of God, then the kingdom of God has come upon you"** (Matt 12:28). The actual practice of waging spiritual war must be accomplished through the Holy Spirit. Jesus said the Spirit would **"convict the world concerning sin, and righteousness, and judgment"** (John 16:8). As individuals, the path of spiritual maturity begins with conviction of sin. It leads to our receiving Christ Himself as our righteousness. As Christ dwells within us, judgment is manifested against the enemy.

We must see that it is Christ in us who initiates our war against hell. Those who warn against immature Christians engaging in spiritual warfare are correct. To succeed, we must wage a *holy* war. As we have participated with the Holy Spirit in the transformation of our souls, so also are we joined with Him as He leads us into confrontational warfare. By this He manifests the word of divine judgment against **"the ruler of this world"** (John 16:11).

Please also note that Jesus said the Spirit would convict the world concerning sin. This is important. Judgment begins first with the household of God. However, the same Holy Spirit who has transformed us enlists us to transform society. And in His war against the devil, the same pattern which captured us is used against the world. Thus, the Holy Spirit brings conviction to a city; He establishes righteous attitudes in the soul of that city; and to the degree the community turns toward God, Satan is displaced in the heavenly places.

Therefore, as we discern the strongholds over our cities, we ask the Spirit to bring conviction to our society concerning these specific sins. During one of our city prayer times, we prayed that the Holy Spirit would convict drug dealers of sin. We even asked that He would make them fearful, so they would come tearfully to

God for help. A few days later I received a call from a man who had been selling drugs. He was crying, desperate, and scared. He reported that a number of drug dealers in the city had similar feelings; some had even decided to take financial losses and leave. He himself had been a Christian and was backslidden. Today this man is a thankful member of our congregation. Now when he cries, his tears are tears of joy at the wonderful mercies of God.

Along with divine conviction of sin, we pray that the Holy Spirit would bring righteousness into the thoughts and attitudes of the secular leaders. We intercede for governmental agencies to judge and act with righteous judgments, praying for specific individuals to come to know Christ. We pray the same way for the newspaper and local television. In that regard, we have seen the paper swing toward a more conservative profile. In an editorial, they actually commended an anti-satanism demonstration we held in a downtown park on Halloween. Do not just lament the condition of the communications media; intercede for them, praying that the Holy Spirit would convict them of sin and inspire righteousness in their attitudes.

The third phase or arena of warfare the Holy Spirit engages in is judgment: **"because the ruler of this world has been judged"** (John 16:11). It is part of the Holy Spirit's ministry to bring God's judgment against demons, principalities and powers. Satan has already been disarmed and rendered powerless, defeated at the cross of Christ (see Colossians 2:15; Hebrews 2:14; 1 John 3:8). The Holy Spirit conveys this eternal reality, granting authority to the church to establish God's will on earth as it is in heaven.

Some churches in our city have come together as a result of our war against the spirit of antichrist. The antichrist spirit divides Christians over minor doctrinal issues. One of the pastors with whom we pray felt the Lord wanted to bring healing between the Pentecostals and Baptists in town. Following his lead, we repented of spiritual pride concerning the gift of tongues, asking God to direct us to our Baptist friends.

That very evening, as I was looking for a used computer to purchase, I called a classified ad in the paper. Although the man who had placed the ad introduced himself as a Baptist pastor, I had forgotten our prayer. The following morning I went to his house. After an hour or so of computer talk, I stood to leave.

Suddenly, the Baptist pastor asked, "What is God doing?"

I finally remembered our prayer! Tears filled my eyes as the presence of the Lord entered the room. I told him that, just the day before, we had asked God to lead us, and that as charismatics and Pentecostals we had repented for allowing the gifts of the Spirit to divide us from other Christians.

"Wait!" he exclaimed. "I was just with the Baptist pastors in town telling them how we needed more of the gifts of the Spirit like the Pentecostals!"

The next week this pastor was united with us in prayer, and two weeks later we were praying with him at his church. In time, he brought another Baptist pastor, a wonderful brother, into the prayer fellowship. It is significant that the first pastor's name is Paul Widen, for we feel God surely wants to widen our vision of the church.

This is the ministry of the Holy Spirit. Our warfare is never to be fought with human might or natural power. Only as the Spirit of the Lord works with us do we see the church rebuilt and victory come. God wants us directed into Spirit-led prayer that confronts the strongholds of the city, utilizing the power of the Holy Spirit as our weapon.

Dry Bones or a Great Army?

One obstacle we must overcome is the illusion that we, because of our ability to "divide the word," are more spiritual than other churches. This delusion works on many churches concurrently and separates congregations throughout a city. Thus, we remain divided, isolated by our own spiritual pride. But, as God delivers us from our arrogance, we see that we are without understanding when we compare ourselves to ourselves. We are not called to judge one another but to "love one another."

What God is doing today is much like the restoration of the Jews from their Babylonian captivity. Under the threat of warfare, and in spite of discouragement, the Jews were rebuilding the temple. Nehemiah instructed the workers to carry a building tool in one hand and a sword in the other (see Nehemiah 4:17). If one section of the wall came under attack, a trumpet sounded, and all rallied to defend that area.

It must be the same for us. Many times the enemy has been able to defeat a particular church only because the rest of the citywide church was indifferent or unaware of the battle. In this context, we must perceive that it takes a citywide church to win the citywide war.

I hear the reply: "The churches in our city are dead, and we alone are left." Such was Elijah's lament, but the Lord assured him there were yet seven thousand who were faithful. Ezekiel also thought he stood alone, but God brought him out to a valley of dry bones and commanded him to prophesy, to speak to those bones. *After* the bones came together, then the Spirit entered; and, behold, they were **"an exceedingly great army"** (Ezek 37:10).

One of the sins of the church is that we criticize the dry bones, judging them for being lifeless. Yet we fail simply to *speak* to them. There are thousands of pastors and churches that only need to be spoken to and connected with others in the body. God is indeed preparing an exceedingly great army. Through it He intends to pull down the strongholds in the cities. However, they must be *connected in Christ* before the Spirit will anoint them for effective spiritual warfare.

Please hear me. We are fully supportive and thank God for national days of prayer and regional weeks of supplication, and we are calling tens of thousands to pray for specific areas to change. These strategies are essential for loosening the enemy's grip over an area. But if we want to see Satan's kingdom fall, the church must be united. For if the city church is bound and divided by strife, the enemy in that region will not be plundered.

When we pray against the spiritual forces of wickedness over a region, our first line of offense is to pray for the churches to be united in their worship and their warfare. Why pray for the church? The Scriptures tell us that

> **the adversary and the enemy could enter the gates ... Because of the sins of her prophets and the iniquities of her priests** (Lam 4:12-13).

Indeed, if there is **"jealousy and selfish ambition"** in the church, there will inevitably be **"disorder and every evil thing"** in that locality (James 3:16).

Therefore, we conclude: It takes a citywide church to win the citywide war. Our individual evangelistic programs, our Sunday teachings and our aggressive attempts to bind the enemy are of limited value if we, the born-again church, remain divided. One person's transformation from carnality to the image of Christ can revolutionize a church; the transformation of the citywide church into the image of Christ can revolutionize a city.

Let's pray. *Lord Jesus, forgive me for being so independent that I failed to see the needs of the other churches in my city. You said that a house divided cannot stand. You also said that if we are not gathering with You in spiritual warfare, we are actually against You. Lord, I repent of being isolated. I ask You to equip me to be a strength and a help to my brethren throughout the city. Grant me grace, Lord Jesus, to fulfill this prayer to Your glory. Amen.*

Discipleship Training booklets

truths compiled from the writings of Francis Frangipane
$2.50 each, 10 or more—40% discount
50 or more—50% discount

Place order with **Arrow Publications**
P.O. Box 10102, Cedar Rapids, IA 52410
Phone: 319-373-3011 (VISA or MC only)
or FAX: 319-373-3012